Warrior Princess

Becky Clayton-Anderson
&
Shoni Anderson

Tampa, Florida

Warrior Princess

Published by Gatekeeper Press
7853 Gunn Hwy, Suite 209
Tampa, FL 33626
www.GatekeeperPress.com

Copyright © 2023 by Shoni Anderson and Becky Anderson
All rights reserved. Neither this book, nor any parts within it may be sold or reproduced in any form or by any electronic or mechanical means, including information storage and retrieval systems, without permission in writing from the author. The only exception is by a reviewer, who may quote short excerpts in a review.

Library of Congress Control Number: 2023938114

ISBN (hardcover): 9781662940668
ISBN (paperback): 9781662940675

Shoni and I want to thank God for walking through this battle with us. #Godsgotthis was our battle cry many days.

We are so thankful for her dad and my husband, Jeff, as well as all her amazing siblings.

A big thank you to all our family and friends. We are blessed with a huge support system.

We want to thank all the medical staff who cared for Shoni, especially Dr. Gregory Brandt.

And lastly, as her mom, I want to thank Shoni for her bravery and the spirit of a true Warrior Princess. I've witnessed courage and faith of an amazing young woman who inspires me daily with her strength.

I am a warrior princess
and I have cancer.

I was a normal child,
living a normal life.

One day, my legs started to hurt badly.
I didn't understand why they hurt so much.

My mom tried to get answers from different doctors.

One day, in the emergency room, the doctor said I have leukemia.

My mom tried to hide it, but I could tell she was scared.

I knew my mom
and dad would make sure
I was taken care of.

It's been a long road with
a lot of tough days, but
my mom says that I'm
a warrior princess and
I will beat leukemia —
and I believe her.

When I get scared,
my mom and I pray.

God tells me I'm
a warrior princess.

I know God will take
care of me.

My friends and my
teachers have cheered me
along the way.

I'm happy on days
that I'm able to go to school
and play with my friends.

One day, I will be done
with leukemia.

One day, I will ring the bell and not have to take medicine every night.

I am a warrior princess.

As the mother of a child battling cancer, Becky strives to help others in the same situation. She and her daughter, Shoni, have spent countless hours together in the hospital having conversations they never would have had the opportunity to have if Shoni had not been diagnosed with leukemia.

If the story of Shoni's battle and Becky's perspective as her parent can help just one family, then their dream for Warrior Princess
will be a success.

www.ingramcontent.com/pod-product-compliance
Lightning Source LLC
LaVergne TN
LVHW072023060526
838200LV00058B/4661